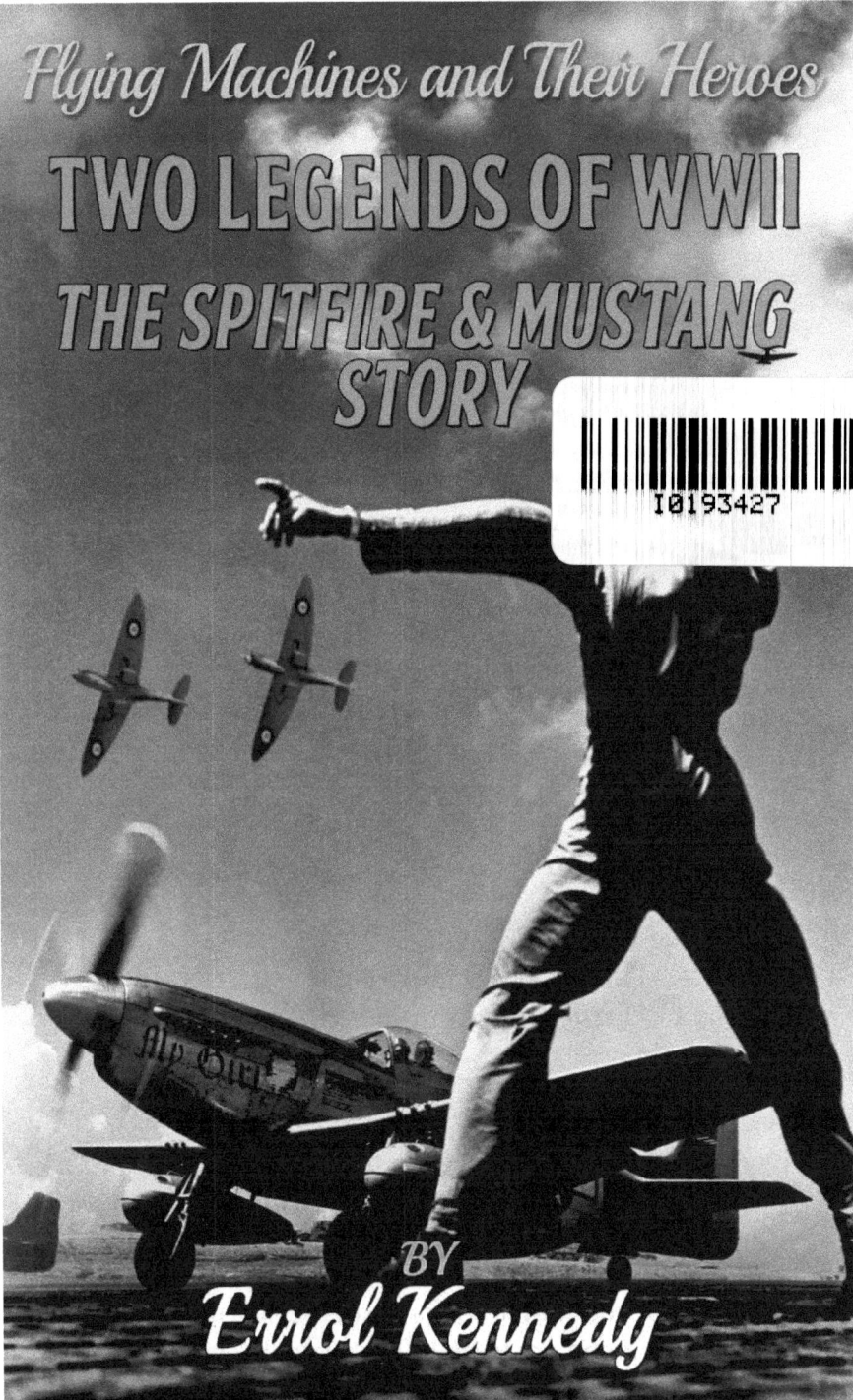

First edition 2015
Published by Lundarien Press, UK
Copyright © Errol Kennedy & Imagination Band Ltd 2015

ISBN 978-1-910816-33-2

The right of Errol Kennedy to be identified as the author of this work has been asserted in accordance with the Copyright, Designs and Patents Act 1988

For more info and other books in this series, including this audiobook read by Robert Powell, go to:

flyingmachinesandtheirheroes.com

Other Books in the
Flying Machines and Their Heroes Series

1. THE BLENHEIM BOMBER STORY
2. AGAINST ALL ODDS - The Guinea Pig Story
3. BY DAY AND NIGHT - The B17 and Lancaster Bomber Story
5. THE PISTON WARRIORS OF WWII

...more to follow soon

Contents

THE SPITFIRE AND MUSTANG STORY   7

Appendix 1 - The Battle of Britain and the   41
               Advance of Radar

Appendix 2 - The Tuskegee Airmen   45

THE SPITFIRE AND MUSTANG STORY

The Super Marine Spitfire is probably the most famous fighter aircraft in the world. It became a symbol of British strength, hope and defiance during the years of World War II and came to symbolise British victory. Certainly no other fighter was more deserving of its place amongst the famous. In its 40 major variants, it was built in greater numbers than any other British aircraft ever. It flew and fought on every single battlefront and in every major

air action during the war. Historically, its finest hour being the Battle of Britain.

Winston Churchill: *"The attitude of every home in our island, in our Empire, and in indeed throughout the world, except in the abodes of the guilty, goes out to the British airmen, who undaunted by odds, unwearied in their constant challenge and mortal danger are turning the tide of the world war by their promise and by their devotion. Never in the field of human conflict was so much owed by so many to so few."*

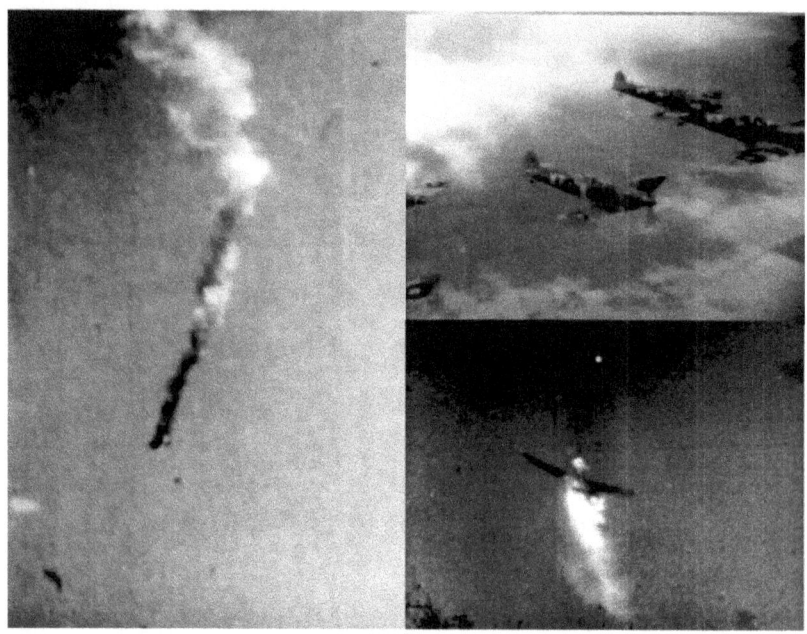

The success of the Spitfire was no accident. Like most of the world's greatest aircraft, the Spitfire was born of an inspired design and the outcome of a lengthy process of technical development.

It was designed from Supermarine's long line of Schneider trophy winning seaplanes. Supermarine had won the Schneider trophy for three

consecutive contests, in 1927, 1929 and 1931, and

several times their planes broke world speed records for floatplanes. The story of the Spitfire began when the Air Ministry issued specification F7 / 30 for a new fighter to replace the ageing Bristol Bulldog which could do no more than 174 mph. At this time the nation was in the middle of a slump and times were very hard for the British aircraft industry.

Consequently there was fierce competition for the contract. Many widely differing designs were built, including five bi-planes. Supermarine designed the type 224 the low winged monoplane of all metal construction, a great novelty at the time. It was powered by a new Rolls Royce 600hp Goshawk engine. However the evaporative cooling system of the Goshawk failed to work properly with the single wing of the monoplane.

In biplanes the steam condenser had been in the upper wing and gravity then pulled the water into the collector tank and then the engine. The low level in the single wing on the 224 meant a lot of adaptations had to be made, but they failed to cool the Goshawk.

The designers also said later that they had been

too cautious with the wing because they had been so worried about flutter, they made it too thick.

The prototype speed of 238mph was not sufficient to justify the Air Ministry trying to iron out the problems and the order was given to the Gloucester, a bi-plane.

Mitchell persuaded Vickers, now owners of Supermarine, otherwise, and for a very short period of time Vickers funded design work themselves.

Rolls Royce was developing its new engine, the PV12, later to be named the Merlin. This used the wing-leading edge of the condenser and they offered this to Supermarine for the new plane. On this basis, the Government then provided £10,000 for the construction of a new prototype to be ready in October 1935. The team was faced with a mass of conflicting requirements which had to be reconciled to produce the most effective compromise. The structure had to be as light as possible and yet strong and rigid enough for great manoeuvrability. Consequently the most critical and ingenious development was the thin wing, which also had to be very strong to avoid flutter.

The wing shape had to change to allow for the weight of the Merlin engine, which was about one third more than the Goshawk. Consequently the centre of gravity in the wing was moved back from the leading edge. They were now more daring about the wing itself, and the new elliptical wing, the feature that makes the Spitfire so distinctive, was proved to be far more superior aerodynamically.

 Mitchell is quoted as saying, "I don't give a bugger what it looks like as long as it covers the guns". The ellipse was the shape that allowed the thinnest possible wing with enough room to carry the arms. The route of the wing was thick enough to accommodate the undercarriage but tapered slowly towards the tips. Beverley Shanstone, Mitchell's aerodynamicist said, "the ellipse was an ideal shape, theoretically a perfection and it looked nice too."

The prototype first flew on the 6th March 1936, Mitchell was by now, desperately ill with cancer. He died in 1937 and the chief draughtsman, Joseph Smith, saw the Spitfire into production.

The Air Ministry issued the first contract for 310 planes at a cost of £4,500 each in 1936. It was the first all metal, stretch-skinned aircraft to be put into quantity production. It was also like other wartime aircraft, largely built by hand.

The alloy skins, flush riveted to reduce drag, informed a strong frame capable of withstanding 10g. In June 1938 squadron 19 received the first Spitfires. When war broke out in September 1939, 9 RAF squadrons were flying Spitfires.

On August 13th 1940, the Germans began 'Eagle attack' the invasion of Britain.

Hitler was confident of victory within two weeks. He had already defeated the Polish and the French forces and had 3,500 aircraft loaded against the RAF's 1,065. Dornier 17s, Messerschmitt 110s and 109s as well as bombers, fought the Spitfires,

Mustangs and Hurricanes of the allies over the skies of Britain. Both the German Dornier 17s and the twin engine Messerschmitt 110 destroyer fighter were, although heavily armed, cumbersome and slow. It was only their similar engine Messerschmitt 109 fighter that could match the speed and manoeuvrability of the Spitfire. It had been a captured Messerschmitt 109 that had partly inspired North American's design of the Mustang.

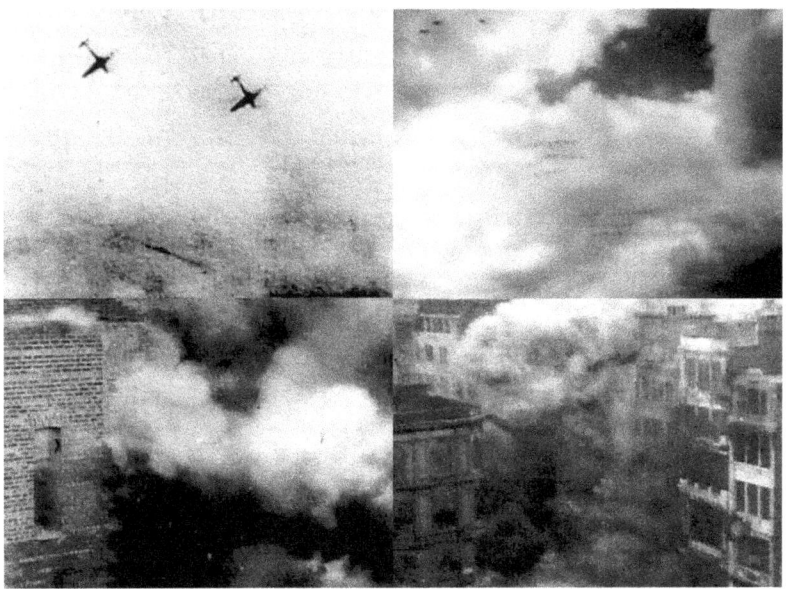

The German bombers attacked every day throughout the summer of 1940 and every day the fighters would fend off both the bombers and their fighter escorts in dogfights.

1,733 German aircraft both bombers and fighters were lost and the Luftwaffe eventually retreated in October 1940. Most of these pilots had only had about 10 hours training to accomplish complex manoeuvres. Only 1000 RAF pilots flew and fought; 451 were killed, 915 aircraft were lost but the German invasion of Britain had been defeated. It was the Battle of Britain that gave the Spitfire immense worldwide fame.

Bob Rahn: "We were the first American group in Europe in World War II and we didn't have any aeroplanes, we left all our aeroplanes in the USA and General Arnold said, 'Get those guys over to Europe by the next boat!' So there we were over in England having a great time chasing all the English girls all over the place and Arnold said, 'Get those guys Spitfires and put them to work.'

"I heard this German shooting at me, I actually heard the machine gun fire and I looked behind me and I saw the biggest damned radial engine I ever saw in my life was on a Focke-Wulfe. I broke hard right, just as hard and fast as I possibly could and I went off and snapped into a spin and once I recovered from the spin I was on his tail."

The public rallied round in tremendous force to raise money for Spitfires throughout the war from putting on shows to fruit picking.

The price of a Spitfire had been fixed at £5,000 although they actually cost twice that amount. In the first two months of 1941 alone, £10m had been raised by the public and 900 more Spitfires had been produced. Supermarine's two factories at East Leigh and Hitchin were bombed. Most of the equipment was saved though and production was replanned and dispersed throughout the country.

A much greater labour force was required; men and women from all professions and walks of life became deployed in the building of Spitfires. All the 900 Mark 2s and Mark 9s were produced at Castle Bromwich.

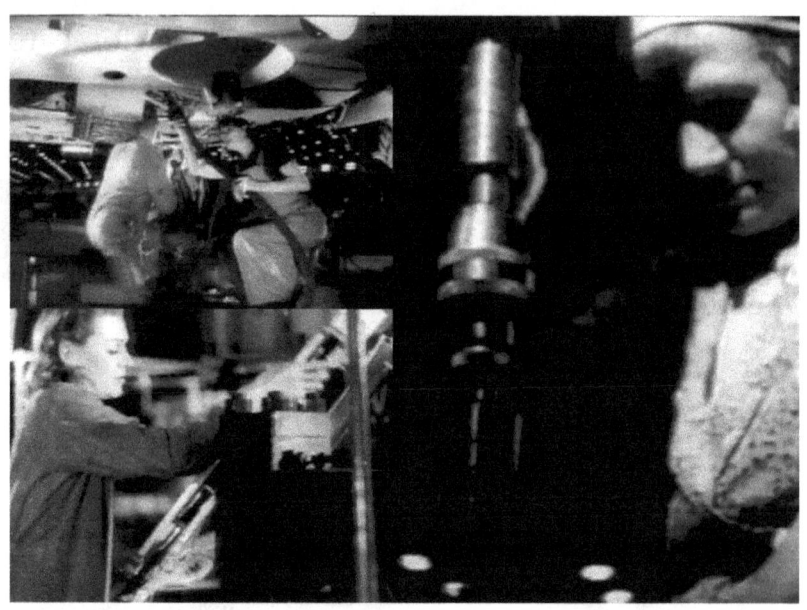

Early Spitfires required 2,400 rounds of .303" ammunition for its eight Browning machine guns. The 300 round magazines were fitted from below

each wing; access to the gun breaches was from above. Armouries could rearm a Spitfire in less than ten minutes.

Each gun hole was covered with canvas to stop it getting clogged before combat and to keep the guns from freezing at altitude. It was soon decided that the weight of shot from the Brownings was inadequate and four of the eight Brownings were replaced with two 20mm Hispano Cannons belt fed with 120 rounds. 30 Mark 1Bs were the first to use the cannon; this combination was called the C wing.

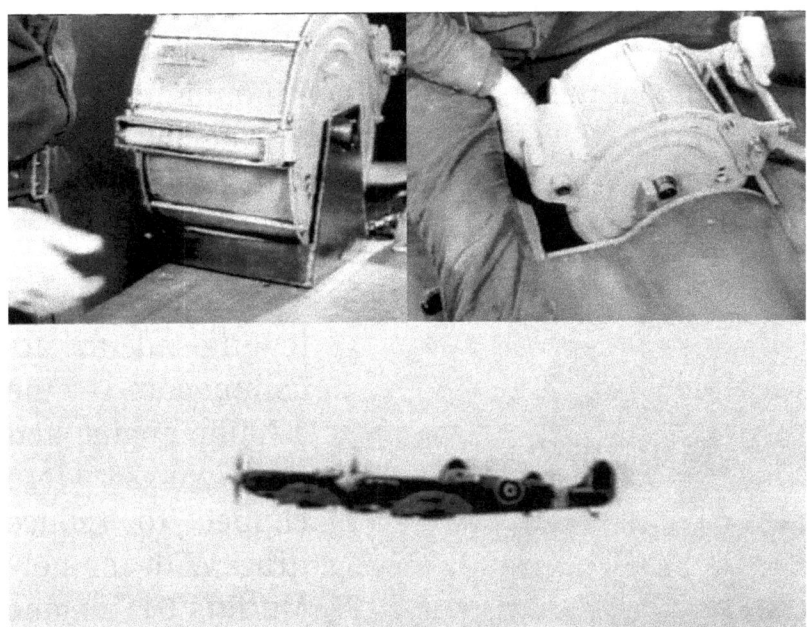

The E wing was introduced on the Mark 9 where in heavier .5 Brownings replaced the .303s to supplement the cannons. Later Marks were fitted with 4 cannons and no machine guns.

Each Spitfire was fitted with a G42 16mm cine gun camera, which automatically filmed when each gun was fired. This was to monitor how many enemy planes had been shot down.

The first major development was the Mark 5, which housed a more powerful Merlin engine. By the start of 1941 it was the Mark 5 that was in service. The next major modifications were made after the Germans introduced their Focke-Wulfe190 powered with a BMW radial engine with 1140 hp. The Focke-Wulfe 190 could travel at 408 mph and the Spitfire was outclassed. To meet the challenge of the Focke-Wulfe with minimum delay, the Merlin 61 was fitted to a Mark 5 airframe to produce the Spitfire Mark 9 with a top speed of 416 miles per hour in high altitude form.

The nose was lengthened to accommodate the 1700hp engine and the wings were clipped to reduce drag. With the new Merlin 61 engine the Spitfire could now perform at high altitude and now its short-range limitations were to be overcome by adding external 30-gallon fuel tanks. It was now able to escort the bombers deeper into enemy territory.

The lengthening of the nose of the aircraft to accommodate the bigger and bigger engines was slightly detrimental to its handling and the nose had always impaired landing visibility.

Captain Bob Beardsley, WW2 Spitfire pilot: "You must get the tail up as soon as possible by pushing the stick forward, bags of boost, and landing is a matter of approach from a turn into the end of the runway rather than how they do it now which is straight down. We used to get as close to the runway as we could and then side slip it in like that; you could do it with a Spitfire, especially if there was a cross wind and then land it on the runway and at the last minute get the tail down."

Sqn. Ldr. Ray Hanna, A.F.C & bar Leader Red Arrows '65-'68: "If the ground view is very poor when you are taxiing, you have to weave the nose from side to side to make sure you know where you are going and that you are not going to hit anything. That is all part and parcel of flying these high-powered tail wheeled aeroplanes. You will have seen in film from the war years Spitfires making curved approaches right to the last minute when they roll the wings level and touch down, Ideally in one

smooth movement, so on the curved approach you can see the airfield and the planned landing run on the final approach."

The narrow undercarriage and poor landing visibility made it unusable as a naval plane as it could not land on the small decks of the aircraft carriers. Developed continuously throughout the war, the Spitfire and its naval counterpart, the Sea Fire, were at some point deployed on every allied front, not solely as fighters but also as reconnaissance and patrolling and even as bombers.

Sqn. Ldr. Ray Hanna: "All the Merlin powered Marks are much the same, they all fly in much the same manner. People like Johnny Johnson have said and will say that the Mark 9 was the best of the Merlin powered variants. From the 12 onwards excluding the 16 which was another Merlin, they are all Griffin powered aeroplanes, instead of

having about 1500hp or 1600hp, they have over 2000hp and because there is that much more power and more power to be absorbed by the propeller, the aeroplanes a little bit more difficult to fly as there is a larger torque effect and any power change means a trim change. So the reason why people like Johnny Johnson said the Mark 9 was better was probably because as a gun platform, it was better."

Captain Bob Beardsley: "The noses of the Spitfires got a bit longer due to more power and the hoods got larger, the first ones were small canopies, then they started bubbling them to get better vision. They were much more responsive as a result, then you got three bladed props, then you got four bladed props, it all helped a lot."

Of the 20,334 Spitfires built in the 18 variants between 1937 and 1945. Some 140 remain today in museums or private collections throughout the world.

Captain Bob Beardsley: "Its immediately responsive, its not an aeroplane that flies itself. You must trim it correctly so that it flies with as little pressure on you as possible. Its very sensitive and immediately responsive aeroplane but had no vices. Not that I found out anyway."

Tim Wallace, founder of the Alpine Flight Collection: "The Spitfire is so well balanced, it feels like you wear a Spitfire like a pair of gloves, it fits perfectly, its made for the pilot. "

Sqn. Ldr. Ray Hanna: "Well from the pilots point of view its probably perfect or as near perfect as any aeroplane can be.

Its essentially vice-less".

Perhaps the last word should come from the Royal Canadian Air forces pilot officer J.G. Magee. In a poem he wrote shortly before his death in 1941, called an Airman's Ecstasy.

"Oh I have slipped the surly bonds of earth
And danced the skies on laughter silvered wings,
Sunward I have climbed and joined the tumbling
    mirth
Of sun-split clouds and done a hundred things
You have not have dreamed of. Wield and soared and
    swung
High in the sunlit silence hovering there.
I chased the shouting wind along and flung
My eager craft through footless halls of air.
Up, up the long delirious blue,

*I topped the windswept heights with easy grace,
Where never lark nor even eagle flew,
And wild with silent lifting mind I've trod
The high untrespassed sanctity of space,
Put out my hand and touched the face of God."*

Former RAF Squadron Leader Rod Dean: "Really a lot of people look at the Spitfire as being the fighter of the Second World War and of course it was certainly as far as the British were concerned, and the Mustang really holds the same place in terms of the Americans.

The North American Mustang was unquestionably the finest of all the United States Air Forces fighters.

Unlike the Spitfire the Mustang was almost designed by accident. As Britain entered the war Chamberlain, the RAF and the Air Ministry knew they did not have enough aircraft to fight the Nazi onslaught.

In 1940 a delegation from the British Government

went shopping to the United States for fighter aircraft. They initially asked Curtis for a replacement for the ageing P40s but Curtis could not guarantee delivery until the end of 1940.

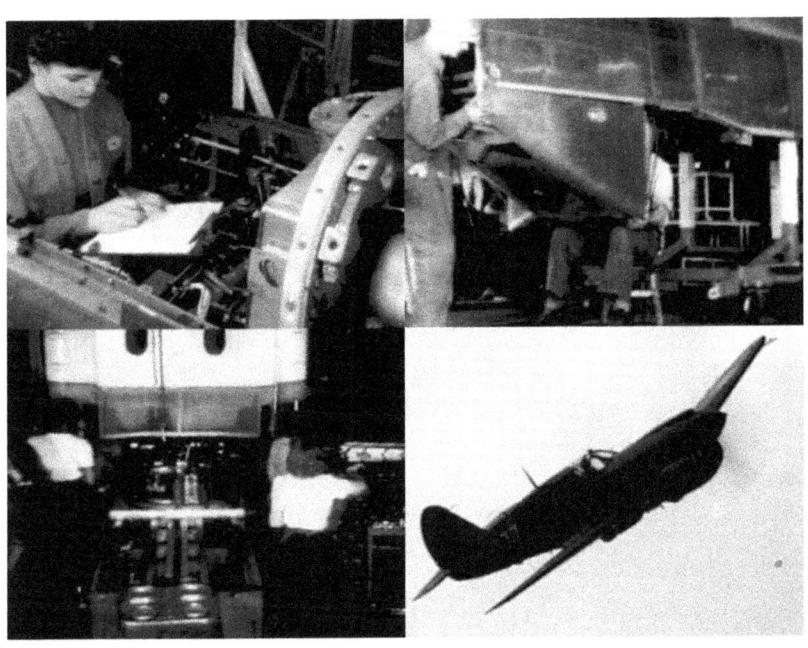

North America were then approached instead with the requirement that a prototype fighter must be produced within 120 days. They were furnished with all the latest RAF fighter specifications plus a detailed report on a captured Messerschmitt 109.

Under the charismatic leadership of their boss, James H Dutch Kindleberger, the company set to their task at full force.

The prototype was

produced in record time and was first flown on October 26th 1940. The name Mustang came from the British Purchasing Commission. Evaluation by the British confirmed the enthusiasm with which the design had been greeted.

Subsequently the British Government increased its order from 320 to 620, the cost to the British taxpayer was some $15M though seldom has money been better spent.

The main goal of the design team was to reduce weight and cut down drag to a minimum. It was decided to use the revolutionary Laminar flow wing. This meant moving the thickest section of the wing towards the middle, unlike conventional designs which concentrated the thickest part of the wing towards the leading edge.

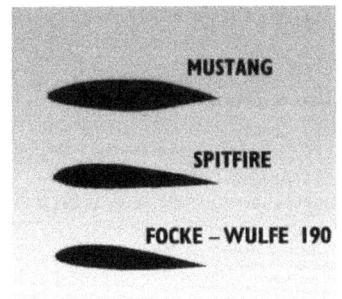

The new Laminar flow profile greatly increased the Mustang's performance and range, primarily through fuel efficiency.

Former RAF Sqr Leader Rod Dean: "But it's a generation later than the Spitfire and you can see that in the many different characteristics of it. It's a heavier aeroplane, its up to 12,000lbs or thereabouts compared to the Spitfires 8,000 and yet on the same engine its 30-40 mph faster. You can see that there has been a different generation of aerodynamics coming into it. It has a Laminar flow wing, its got a lot more fuel than the Spitfire and consequently will go much further and faster, but you do lose out, it won't turn as well as a Spitfire, you've to pay a price for those benefits and the price is in its turn performance."

Lt. Cdr Norman Lees: "The difference to this aircraft, it has a laminar flow wing, it means it is a little less forgiving than a Spitfire."

To further streamline the aircraft, the radiator air intake was moved well back under the fuselage beneath the cockpit area.

Lt. Cdr Norman Lees: "It is a very hot aeroplane, very warm inside, the radiators are right underneath and I would imagine that cruising at 30,000 feet in it across to Berlin and back on a cold winter's night, one would be quite pleased about the heat."

The engine used in the early Mustangs was the Allison, which gave excellent performance at low altitudes, but proved disappointing at the altitudes that most of the combats were being fought over Europe.

Consequently the RAF concentrated fighter development on the Spitfire.

The Mustang had twin fuel tanks in the wings, an auxiliary tank behind the cockpit with the possibility of wing drop tanks.

Norman Chapman, former RAF flight engineer: "On the main tanks in the fuselage in your wings, would give you roughly 1.5 hours to 2 hours range, with your 90 gallon fuselage tank, you would have another 2 hours range and with your drop tanks you would perhaps have a range of about 7 hours."

The fuel tanks were also self-sealing if punctured by gunfire.

"All the tanks were self sealing, apart from the drop tanks but it would only work in the case of small punctures not a 20mm shell going through it. What used to happen was that neoprene was used with an inter-fill of raw rubber. The petrol on the raw rubber would make it swell out and plug the hole which was only say a .303 calibre hole or maybe ¼ inch or ½ inch hole but certainly not 2 inches or anything like that."

This gave the Mustang excellent endurance at low altitudes, which enabled it to range deep into enemy territory. It was therefore used initially as a low level tactical reconnaissance and ground attack aircraft to devastating effect.

The first Mustangs to be used in this role were Mark 1s. These carried four .5" and four .3" machine guns as well as a Neff 24 camera mounted obliquely aft of the cockpit.

By this time the United States Air Force was beginning to equip some of its own squadrons with Mustangs and found it had an additional role as a dive-bomber.

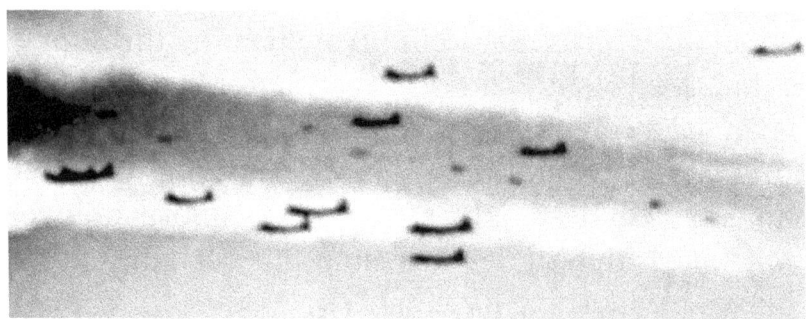

The flying fortresses of the United States Eighth Air Force were now well into their daylight bombing campaigns. However they were suffering terrible loses. This was partly due to the lack of fighter escort; the P47 Thunderbolts and the P38 Lightnings could only carry enough fuel to escort the bomber's part of the way to their targets.

Gen. Curtis Le Mai: "We also planned that we would have fighter escorts and not only that, attack aeroplanes who work over the flack on the missions but we arrived in the war unprepared. We had no bombers, no fighters, nor attack aeroplanes."

Retired L.T.C. Boardman Reed, US Air force: "When we finally got the B17 Fs and started going in deep penetration, we did not have the fighter escorts to go very far; we had P47s but they would only go in a short way and they would have to leave us and the Germans would take over and it scared us to death."

The Bombers were then left to the mercy of the Luftwaffe.

In England some Mustangs were experimentally fitted with the Merlin. Flight tests showed that the aircraft's high altitude

33

performance was phenomenally increased. Speeds of up to 440 miles per hour at 30,000 feet were achieved.

It was realised that this could be the answer to the bomber's long-range escort problem. Details were sent to North America and after their own flight tests were completed the Merlin Mustang was put into full-scale production.

Former RAF Sqr Leader Rod Dean: "If you wanted to go to Berlin and back you would take a Mustang, as a Spitfire would not do it. If you were interested in an aircraft that climbed quickly and was very manoeuvrable, the Spitfire is probably the better of the two."

Both the American fighter groups and the RAF began equipping with the new Mustang Mark 3. They first went into action over Europe in July 1942. The force of the bombers under the full escort of these intrepid and fierce fighters was formidable and the axis powers began to lose control of their own air space. This proved to be the turning point of the war.

Every pilot would have his own combat stories. Bruce Carr's story was a little different: "I was over Czechoslovakia and got hit in the coolant and since I had a little experience bailing out, I trimmed the aeroplane up as well as I could and stepped over the side delayed my parachute opening as long as I dared, landed near the woods; woods in Czechoslovakia and Germany in those days had nowhere to hide because the ground was picked completely clean. The aeroplane crashed far enough away that the Germans did not arrive right away, although there was no doubt they were looking for me. I knew exactly where I was and I was trying to get to Switzerland, but believe me you do not stand a snowball chance in hell of walking that far without food and shelter. So I went to a German airbase to surrender because I was exhausted, cold and hungry and had been down a week.

"I sat in some trees and watched the Germans working on an aeroplane and as they got it fixed, refuelled it and ran it up, the same way we would do things, I decided I would give it a go and get through the wire and go for it.

The wire was a problem but I made it and got into the aeroplane, closed the canopy and sat there until it began to get light; I assumed the Germans did the same thing as we did, that they turned the switches off when they leave the aeroplane and on to start it, so I reversed all the switches in the cockpit and then it got a little lighter and I saw a T-handle down on the right hand side that said "starter" in English so I pulled it and nothing happened.

Perhaps I swore I don't remember but anyway I pushed the handle down and the starter started grinding up, I pulled it and it fired right up and I knew where the field was so I taxied there as fast as I dare through the woods and as soon as I saw the field I turned left and gave it full throttle and took off."

The Mustangs not only dominated the European skies, they were also deployed in the Mediterranean and Pacific. It was the Mustang that escorted super fortresses over the Japanese mainland. The Mustang went through a number of further revisions during the war including the unique P82 or twin Mustang.

The final version of the Mustang the B51H proved to be the fastest, it achieved speeds of 487mph at 30,000ft.

Former RAF Sqr Leader Rod Dean: "From a handling point of view there's

37

no doubt about it, the Spitfire is probably the better of the two in terms of pure handling and being on the pilots side. The Mustangs got some characteristics again because of the aerodynamics, particularly in the stall area, which were not particularly good. On the other side of that same coin you can use the flaps for combat. For instance you can lower ten flap up at 410mph, so you can offset some of the stall problems by using flap."

Even under the stress of war it takes a considerable amount of time to apply the lessons of experience to a completely new design. At the rapid genealogical processes through which the Mustang passed, were phenomenal by any standard. The Mustang created records of achievement from the day of its inspired conception up to the day the war ended. It is said to be probably the best all round single piston engine fighter to be deployed by any of the combatants in World War 2.

Flt. Lt. John Peters, a present day pilot: "I was extremely fortunate as it is very rare these days to get the opportunity to be able to sit in the jump seat of a Mustang snuck up in the back and whilst I didn't fly it I very much got the essence of the aircraft, it was as if you strapped the aircraft on, it was very small, rather than a Tornado where you get into the aircraft itself and it was very much a gutsy feeling, maybe more personal really, like a man and machine together at a basic stage, whereas Tornado is man and computer and that's a very different attitude of mind."

Former RAF Sqr Leader Rod Dean: "The Spitfire is a generation earlier and it shows that its also a light aeroplane with a big engine, whereas the Mustang is a big heavy aeroplane with the right sized engine for it. The Spitfire has a narrow track undercarriage which does make its ground handling a little more tricky than the Mustangs. The Mustang has a big wide track undercarriage and steerable tail wheel that does help on the ground."

Flt. Lt John Peter: "Obviously flying Tornado is my job but it was the essence of flying when your flying a Mustang."

In all 14,819 Mustangs were produced and in the war over Europe the Mustang is credited with the shooting down of nearly 5,000 enemy aircraft.

There are around 200 Mustangs still in existence, with many of them continuing to fly, restored by enthusiasts from all over the world.

Lt. Cdr Norman Lees: "This aircraft in particular was taken down to its very basic components almost every rivet removed and then each individual component treated, resprayed and put back together again. Once you have done that to an aeroplane to keep it going for another fifty years provided you have the spares resources and also obviously the financial resources as well."

Although the majority of the 200 survivors reside in the USA, P51s also exist in many other countries ranging from Britain to Israel, The Philippines, China, Korea, Australia and New Zealand. In private collections or in museums, and airframes are still being restored today.

APPENDIX 1
THE BATTLE OF BRITAIN AND THE ADVANCE OF RADAR

After the fall of France and the Low Countries in June 1940, Adolf Hitler looked next to conquer the rebellious British force, still under the control of Sir Winston Churchill. Britain was ruling the waves and in 1940 the Royal Navy was the best in the world. Only the English Channel lay between Germany's continental conquests and the British Isles. Luftwaffe Reichsmarshal Herman Goering supported and aided Hitler's decision to bomb the British into submission, before attempting a cross-channel invasion. Hitler gave Goering the all clear to reduce the British resistance from the air. It seemed like a ludicrous decision as Germany's air power had already been tested in the past and had not lived up to expectations.

The Germans went ahead despite the poor condition of the Luftwaffe to pursue such a conflict. Unfortunately for them the German twin-engine bombers did not have the range or bomb load capacity required to engage battle sufficiently. Luftwaffe forces were also tired and worn down from their previous missions and more importantly German fighters lacked the range to offer adequate fighter coverage for their bombers.

The British had been preparing an aerial defence since 1937, under the direction of Air Marshal Sir

Hugh Dowding. Whilst short of pilots, England had almost 700 new Spitfires and Hurricanes that were made available in June 1940. It was the Mk. 1 Spitfire that bore the brunt of fighting during the Battle of Britain. What's more, by late 1940, under the direction of Lord Beaverbrook, the British aircraft industry was producing an astonishing 400 fighters a month, compared to 200 per month by the Germans.

On July 10, 1940, the Battle of Britain began with Luftwaffe attacks on convoys within the English Channel. The purpose of the attacks was not only to destroy and disrupt British shipping but to invite the RAF into battle so as to destroy their force in the air. Through mid-August, Germany attacked British airfields and radar stations. They were confident that they were wearing down the RAF, when in fact the opposite was actually happening. The British air defence system was all together more advanced and equipped than the enemy. Radar stations provided RAF Fighter Command with details on approaching German aircraft who in turn gave instructions to Sector, Group, and Squadron commanders to act upon. The detection and location of aircraft by radio beams had made rapid progress since the first experiments that took place in February 1935. Five years later a chain of coastal radar stations were set up covering the east and south sides of the country. At 10,000 feet, enemy aircraft could be detected at ranges of 50-120 miles. Additional radar stations were built to cater for low-flying aircraft so that they could be detected at 1,000 feet and below. Radar was one of the most important factors to the success of the air defences during the Battle of Britain. The Germans were not fully aware of the full potential that radar had achieved and therefore did not place the highest of priorities on its destruction.

On August 13 1940 the Luftwaffe launched a major attack on RAF airfields under the code-name Adlertag (Eagle Day). Poor weather conditions and ferocious RAF fighter defence hampered the Luftwaffe bombers from doing too much damage. Losing only 13 fighters, the RAF shot down 45 Luftwaffe aircraft. The Germans continued to concentrate on the RAF for the next month only to be frustrated by their inability to destroy them. On September 5, the Germans decided to switch to night bombing. This movement initiated the beginning of the Blitz which saw casualties rise as its pace increased. The greatest threat had actually passed unknown to the British people and whilst the blitz continued, the RAF grew stronger in mind and machine. The Battle of Britain ended on 31st October 1940.

One of the great British aces of the Battle of Britain was a gentleman named Douglas Bader who lost both his legs while flying a Bristol Bulldog from Kenley to Woodley airfield in 1931. The doctors had to amputate, and Bader was not expected to live, but as a true hero, he survived, and with the aid of tin legs, began flying again. He was grounded for the next several years, but after war broke out he was back flying the skies. He quickly rose to command 222 Squadron, and by June of 1940 was in command of 242 Squadron, the only Canadian squadron in the RAF at the time. On August 9, 1941, his luck ran out when he collided with a Messerscmitt Bf 109. He was captured by the Germans and taken to the infamous Colditz castle.

General Adolf Galland one of Germany's most famous aces cooperated in delivering to Douglas Bader a pair of artificial legs that were airdropped by the British into France. Bader survived the war and was knighted in 1976 by Queen Elizabeth for his services to amputees. He sadly passed away in 1982.

APPENDIX 2
THE TUSKEGEE AIRMEN

In July 1941, the Army Air Corps began a program to train Black Americans as military pilots. Until that time, Blacks had been forbidden to receive pilot training. The military selected the Tuskegee Institute to train pilots because of its commitment to aeronautical training. The program was named the 'Tuskegee Experiment'.

Once cadets had completed primary training they were sent to nearby Tuskegee Army Air Field to complete flight training and transition to combat type aircraft. Enlisted members were trained to be aircraft and engine mechanics, armament specialists, radio repairmen, parachute riggers, control tower operators, policemen, administrative clerks and all of the other skills necessary to fully function as an Army Air Corp flying squadron or ground support unit.

The Tuskegee Airmen were dedicated, determined young men who enlisted to become America's first black military airmen, at a time when there were many people who thought that black men lacked intelligence, skill, courage and patriotism. They came from every section of the country, with large numbers coming from New York City, Washington, Los Angeles, Chicago, Philadelphia and Detroit. Each one possessed a strong personal desire to serve the US to the best of his ability. Those who possessed the physical and mental qualifications were accepted as aviation cadets to be trained initially as single-engine pilots and later as twin-engine pilots, navigators or bombardiers. They flew more than 15,000 sorties, completing over 1,500 missions during the war. Equipped with their red-tailed P51 Mustangs, their responsibility was to protect the bombers, not to zoom off, hunting enemy planes to shoot down. The 332nd Fighter Group is a case in point; the group's highest scoring pilot was credited with only 4 kills, but they never lost a bomber to enemy fighters.

American bomber crews reverently referred to them as "The Black Red-Tail Angels" because of the identifying red paint on their tail assemblies. The tenacious bomber escort cover provided by the 332nd "Red Tail" fighters often-discouraged enemy fighter pilots from attacking bombers they were escorting. This resulted in fewer enemy fighter challenges with resultant fewer enemy aircraft destroyed or damaged by the Group. The successful escort record resulted in frequent expressions of appreciation from the bomber crews. Feared and respected by the Germans, the Airmen were also known as the "Schwartze Vogelmenschen" which translates to Black Birdmen.

Their bravery in the air and dignity on the ground won them the highest honours. Each Tuskegee Airman accepted the challenge, proudly displayed his skill and determination, whilst concealing internal rage from humiliation caused by regular experiences of racism at home and overseas. Indeed these airmen fought two wars; one against a military force overseas and the other against racism at home and abroad.

At the end of the war the Tuskegee Airmen returned home with numerous awards for gallantry only to face continued racism despite their outstanding war efforts. Tuskegee Army Air Field continued to train new airmen until 1946, with women entering the program in various ways. Large numbers of black airmen elected to remain in the service but because of segregation their assignments were limited to the 332nd Fighter Group or the 477th Composite Group, and later to the 332nd Fighter Wing at Lockbourne Air Base in Ohio. Opportunities for promotion were very limited and this affected morale. Nevertheless, black airmen continued to perform superbly. In 1949 pilots from the 332nd Fighter Group took first place in the Air Force National Fighter Gunnery Meeting at Las Vegas Air Force Base, Nevada.

During this period, many white units were understaffed and needed qualified people to join them, but were unable to get the experienced black personnel because of the segregation policy. The newly formed U.S. Air Force initiated plans to integrate its units as early as 1947. In 1948, President Harry Truman oversaw equality of treatment and opportunity in all of the United States Armed Forces. This in time led to the end of racial segregation in the military forces and was also the first step towards racial integration in the US. The positive experience, the outstanding record of accomplishment and the superb behaviour of black airmen during World War II, and after were important factors towards the initiation of the historic social change to accomplish racial equality in America.

ACKNOWLEDGEMENTS

I would like to thank the following for their part in making this book possible:

The Royal Air Force
Ministry of Defence
Imperial War Museum
RAF Museum, Hendon
Rockwell International Corporation
Vickers
Rolls Royce
Eric Simonson
Brendan Walsh
Steve Manfield
Tracey Power
Alpine Flight Collection Tim Wallis
Spitfire Ace Bob Rahn
Captain Bruce Carr
Captain Bob Beardsley WW2 Spitfire Pilot
Squadron Leader Ray Hanna A.F.C. & Bar Leader Red Arrows
Squadron Leader Rod Dean Q.F.I.
General Curtis Le Mai
Lieutenant Commander Norman Lees R.N.R.
Flt. Lt. John Peters
Flight Engineer Norman Chapman
Julian Ankersmit
Annekin Wild
Sarah Merrill
Steve Connor
J G Magee
Phin Hall

Cover picture by Corbis
Artwork by Stuart Forrester

If you have enjoyed this book, please consider reviewing it on Amazon or Goodreads (or both)

And feel free visit the *Flying Machine And Their Heroes* website for other titles in this series and to receive a free audiobook:

flyingmachinesandtheirheroes.com

www.ingramcontent.com/pod-product-compliance
Lightning Source LLC
Chambersburg PA
CBHW071801040426
42446CB00012B/2664